HOW TO TAKE THE PATH TO FINANCIAL FREEDOM

BY

ANTHONY K. MARCUS

This book is a work of non-fiction. Names and places have been changed to protect the privacy of all individuals. The events and situations are true.

ISBN: 1-4107-8362-6 (e-book)
ISBN: 1-4140-0304-8 (Paperback)

This book is printed on acid free paper.

1stBooks – rev. 08/21/03

TABLE OF CONTENTS

INTRODUCTION

Everyone loves money and everyone needs money, but money is the one subject most of us would rather not discuss. We talk about everything but our financial issues. We all know that having money and being wealthy can bring us joy and happiness, but on the other hand, we also know that not having wealth and money can lead to frustration and misery.

Life is filled with uncertainty and is unpredictable. You never know what is going to happen next. So having the ability to manage your money is one of the most important tasks you must tackle, in order to live a happier, less stressful life. Learning how to take control of your money and understanding that you are the only person who has the power to decide how to use it wisely is the path to financial freedom.

Some say that life is made of dreams.

Without dreams you wouldn't have

anything to strive towards. And, of course,

without money, you wouldn't have the

ability to achieve those dreams. Our

dreams, vision, and intentions in life cannot

be fulfilled without money. Money is the

key therefore; having financial stability is

the first step in achieving your goals and

living a better, healthier life.

The point of this book is to help you make

your dreams a reality and to help you

discover and appreciate your own true

nature more clearly. In today's modern

world, there are all types of information,

knowledge and advice, so why not utilize

them to our advantage to help us improve

our lives and the lives of our loved ones

surround us. Use all the resources available

to you as well as your natural wits and

instincts. Do not underestimate your inner

wisdom. Read on and find out how you

can use your own personal wisdom to start
on the path to financial freedom.

By doing so, you will know precisely what
you want, and perhaps have a better
understanding of your life. You'll be able to
make important decisions more consciously
and more securely. Achieving your goal to
financial freedom is much easier than most
people believe.

CHAPTER ONE

UNDERSTANDING AND TAKING

CONTROL OF YOUR MONEY

KNOW YOUR FINANCIAL STATUS

Many people often find themselves not knowing where their money goes and how much they overspend each month. It is essential to face the facts and know exactly where you stand financially so that you can be in control of your own finances. It might not be easy and extremely time consuming, but think of how much you will gain knowing exactly how you spend your hard earned money, to know whether or not you overspend and to precisely see where you stand right now. It is worth the time and effort.

We can only control all that we know and not the things we don't know. This is precisely the reason why it is so important for us to know our financial status. If you want to gain control of your finances, then you must first know and understand your money. Money is the essence of our social way of life so we need to understand it to help us achieve our goals and make our dreams come true.

COST OF LIVING

First gather all your cash receipts, canceled

checks, credit card bills/statements, and

ATM statements from the past year. Look

through them and make sure you have all of

them within arms reach. After you

rummage through all your financial papers

from the past year, you should have a good,

or at least a better idea of how much you

have spent over the last twelve months.

Now organize those papers by putting them

in separate piles by month—put all the

papers from January in one stack, all of the

ones from February in another and so on.

After sorting them by month, make

categories for each month, such as, food

costs, clothing, utilities, rent/mortgage

payment, telephone, credit card payments,

etc. Then add up all the expenses from each

of the categories of each month and divide

each of the totals by 12. This will tell you

your average expenses per month for each

category. To find your total average cost of

living per month, add up all the averages in

each category. The number you receive will

tell you how much money it's costing you to

live the way you do right now.

MONTHLY INCOME

Now that you know your average cost of

living, you must figure out how much

income you are making and whether or not

you can afford your style of living. This is

the only way you will be able to know

where you stand financially. Start by

calculating your income by writing down all

your income sources and amount of income

you receive from each source. Be as precise

and realistic as possible on how much you

make each month. Don't lie to yourself!

Count all income sources such as monthly

paychecks after taxes, bonuses, investment

income, rental income, pension, social

security, disability income and all other

miscellaneous incomes. Add up all the

income from the various sources and divide

it by 12. Now you have just figured out

your monthly income after having paid your

taxes.

BALANCING YOUR MONEY

Compare your expenses to your incomes.

Now you know where you stand financially.

It's a good feeling to know where you stand

whether you're spending less than you earn

or spending more than you earn and is in

debt like most people are these days. If you

are in debt, you can do two things: (1) find

another source of income and/or (2) start

trimming down on those expenses. Look through all your expense categories one more time. Try to determine how much money you are willing to spend in each category and what category you are able to trim down expenses from. Do not make any unrealistic budget cuts. Reduce the amount of money spent only on the appropriate categories, ones that you can do without. Cut back on those non-essential luxury items. You can live without them. Just try it.

Taking control of your finances may seem impossible, but you can start by following the steps above. There is no better feeling than to know where you are stand financially and having a way to stabilize your finances.

CHAPTER TWO

BEING RESPONSIBLE TO YOUR

LOVE ONES

SELF -DISCIPLINE, MOTIVATION &

POWER OF THE MIND

The road to financial freedom isn't an easy one. It requires action, responsibility and most of all – self discipline. In order to build a strong financial foundation, you need support, emotional support, which your family can give you. Family will give you the will power to take charge of your own lifestyle and be responsible in the ways you spend your money.

Even if you have the ability to be a spendthrift, you will think twice before spending it because of your family's needs,

that is self-discipline. After all, having

money and being wealthy doesn't

necessarily equate to happiness. Money

cannot comfort you when your heart is

broken, but a life rich with the people you

love can. Having a strong family and

emotional foundation will help you build

and maintain your financial structure for

life.

You need motivation to keep you focused on your goal. What can give a person more motivation than one's family and loved ones? If you ever lose the initiative to gain control of your finances, think of your family and how much they need your love and, truth be told, your money. Having financial stability will help you and your loved ones in the long run. Taking responsibility for you and your loved ones will guide your way to financial freedom in the years ahead.

Our state of mind directly affects our approach to our finances. A secure state of mind allows one to think more clearly and responsibly. It allows for better judgments of expenses and the solving of financial problems. Knowing that you have taken care of your loved ones and that they are safe clears your way to achieving financial freedom. Being responsible for family and loved ones helps to stabilize your mind and eventually leads to financial stability.

WILL & LIVING TRUST

The drawing up of a will and a living trust

will help your loved ones in the future.

Plus, it gives you the motivation to secure

your finances so that you can help those you

love in their financial future. It would be

wise to write a will and a living trust now, if

you haven't done so already. It will give

you peace of mind knowing that what you

worked so hard to gain will end up with the

ones you love.

HEALTH CARE INSURANCE

Having a strong and reliable Health care insurance provider now will help you stay out of debt later. Should you or any member of your family suffer any injury or medical condition in the future, you will have the ability to pay for those emergency expenses without burning a hole in your wallet. It will save you from financial grievances later if you or your loved ones are ever in need of medical attention. Make sure to have medical insurance for you

never know what will happen in the future

to you or the ones you love.

POWER OF ATTORNEY FOR

HEALTH CARE

Making arrangement for a Durable Power

of Attorney for health care will greatly

benefit you and your loves one in the future.

While you are still strong and healthy, you

should set this up, so when you ever fall

victim to a serious health condition and is

unable to make critical decisions. You may want certain actions taken if you are ever incapacitated and unable to speak for yourself. Requests could go something like the following:

(1) You want to prolong your life regardless of your condition, whether you are in a coma or in vegetative state.

(2) You want life-sustaining treatment unless you are in a vegetative state, then two attending physicians can

determine the best course of action for

you.

(3)   You want your life to be ended if there

is no chance of recovery, mentally

and/or physically.

LIFE INSURANCE

An affordable life insurance policy is a

worthwhile investment whether you are

young or old. Having life insurance

coverage will help to relieve some of the

financial burdens your loved ones may or

may not have in the event of your death.

There are affordable policies on the market.

A term life insurance policy is the policy

that many would recommend to the average

person. These policies are not very

expensive and are affordable for the

common person. Term Life insurance

policies have a time limit attached to them

and are bought by people as a precaution.

This type of policy has a fair low premium

because the insurance company doesn't

expect you to claim the policy and receive

money any time in the near future. It's the

only reasonable policy to buy for the

ordinary person. You should forget about

those expensive life insurance policies. The

commissions you would have to pay for

these types of life and/or universal policies

are ridiculously high. In fact, they are one

of most lucrative commission in any

business market. If the point of having life

insurance is to have money set aside for

your loved ones when a catastrophe should

occur, then a term life insurance policy is

the way to go.

OTHER INSURANCES

There are other types of insurance you should consider besides life insurance. *Long-term-care* insurance covers all the expenses needed if you were to enter a nursing home or have a current medical condition. You should also buy this insurance now if you are fifty years of age or higher. You never know what could happen in the future. *Long-term-disability* insurance is another type of insurance you should look into. If ever a catastrophe should occur and you are unable to work, you will receive funds to cover some, if not all, your critical daily expenses. Remember that the purpose of having insurance is to help you and your family in the even of a crisis. You should be grateful if you never have to use it. And don't forget to shop around for the lowest premiums available on all insurance policies and talk to the insurance agents for details. It could save you a whole lot of money.

HOW TO TAKE THE PATH TO FINANCIAL

FREEDOM

BEING RESPONSIBLE

By protecting and being responsible of your loved ones now and their future, you have learned one of life's many lessons—putting people above money. Knowing that your loved ones are safe is one of the most fulfilling feelings anyone could ever experience. You are able to remind yourself about who you are and about what is important in life, which is your family.

Taking the steps outlined in this chapter will lead you to knowing how to be a better person and guide you on to the road to financial freedom.

WHAT IS A GOAL

A goal is a projection of one's life's intention. It is a promise you make to yourself, a promise that you strive to fulfill in life. A goal must be precise, explicit, and measurable. It leaves no room for interpretation. A goal is also a promise that you make to yourself about something you want done in your life. It must be something that is attainable. Do not create unattainable, unrealistic goals that can lead you into misery and be discouraging to you.

You must set life goals that demonstrate one or more of your moral standards of integrity. It is relevant to maintain your standards of integrity in order to propel yourself towards meeting your goals. Having good moral judgments is one of the key things in achieving any goal you may

set for yourself.

SETTING FINANCIAL GOALS

Many of us don't set financial goals. There

can be many reasons and excuses why don't

but we just don't make them. Some might

be afraid of failure. Others just don't want

to. Many believe that setting goals takes a

great deal of time and we don't even know

how to set goals. We tell ourselves these

things to rationalize not having set any

goals for ourselves. However setting goals,

financial goals, is something that a person

must do.

We must set our financial goals and

objectives. We must develop plans to

achieve them. The goals provide us with

direction and purpose. It also gives us

motivation and the will power we need to

succeed in our financial future. Without it,

there won't be any financial future for us to

look forward to. Accomplishments in

achieving our financial goals could bring us

happiness and joy that can lead to a better,

healthier life.

CHAPTER THREE

ACHIEVING YOUR FINANCIAL

GOAL

REPSECT YOURSELF AND

YOUR MONEY

M oney is such a large part of our
lives that we develop a close

relationship with it. The relationship we
have with money is the same as the one we
have with people. We seek the bond with
money for the same reason why we seek it
with people. As with yourself and others,
treat your money with great respect. Be
honest with your money. Don't spend
money that you do not have at the moment.
Spend only what you can afford.
Respecting your money is the only way to
keep your money and not repel it away for
you. You disrespect yourself, your loved

ones and your money if you don't plan

wisely for your future. You have to be

honest with your self, face your debt and

invest your money. Remember that money

is magnetic; it attracts only those who

respect it and not those who show

disrespect. If you are respectful of your

money and do what needs to be done with

your money, then you will become a

magnet, attracting all the money you want

to yourself. Who doesn't want to see their

money grow beautifully and bountifully?

Just remember to show your money the

respect it deserves. If you do then more

money will come your way.

Disrespecting your money can show itself in

negative ways. You often lose some of

what you have in your life by neglecting to

pay any attention to it. The way we treat

our money and ourselves touches upon

every aspect of our lives. If you abuse the

money you have, you will end up wasting it

and not have enough for the necessities in

life. This could even include not having

enough to eat or not having any shelter to

live in.

Those people who are respectful to

themselves, respectful of others who have

money as well as those who don't and those

people who are respectful of what money

can and cannot do are said to be people

with a golden touch. However, a golden

touch isn't something you're born with. It

must be learned and understood. Once you

have mastered it, you will lead you to

financial freedom.

CREDIT CARDS

Credit card companies really want your business so they trick you into opening an account by enticing you. They say that you deserve to have credit with their company then eventually hit you with extremely high interest rates that most people can't afford. Consequently, you become highly in debt thanks to the "friendly" credit card companies. If you have a good credit history right now, try to transfer your

highest balances with higher interest to

another credit card company with a lower

interest rate. You might have to deal with

some extra hassles, like doing more

paperwork and making a few more phone

calls, but you won't regret it. Then

concentrate to paying off the smallest

balance first. If you have bad credit right

now, try calling your credit card companies

and asking them to reduce their interest

rates by 3-5 percent. There's no harm in

trying. You may want to seek non-profit

credit counselors to help you eliminate

those high interest rates. By paying a little

more attention to your debt, you will

eventually free yourself from your debt.

Having a credit card can be beneficial or

detrimental to your financial stability

depending on how you use it. Use it only in

cases of emergency or when you know for a

fact that you are able to pay your monthly

credit card bill fully and on time. Be honest

with the amount of money you have and

can afford to use on non-essential prospects.

Respect yourself, your loved ones, and your

money. Don't let money control you. If

you have control over your money then you

have control over your life.

INVESTING YOUR MONEY

You can acquire and accumulate financial

wealth in three main ways. The first one is

by working and earning your money. You

can save up your money little by little.

However, working has its limits. You can

only work until you are at a certain age and

in good health. Once you stop working

you'll stop accumulating money. Another

way is to inherit your money. You can get

money by inheriting it from someone or

some corporation. The problem with that is

that it has drawbacks. Not everyone can

inherit large sums of money from anyone.

So the best way to accumulate and receive

income is to invest your hard earned

money. Invest the money you saved wisely

and let the money work for you. You can

get large amounts of money by investing for

an infinite number of years. Let your

investment(s) grow and treat it with respect

and, eventually, the money will take care of

you and your loved ones.

Whether you are rich or poor, you must

invest. It doesn't matter if it's in your *401k*

or any other type of investment; the key is

"invest" and the more the better. Most

people often think they cannot afford to

invest even a small amount of money; the

fact is that if you try, it is actually easier

than you think.

Start respecting yourself, your loved ones

and your money. Plan your future wisely

and take control of your money. Invest in

IRAs, 401k or other retirement plans that

are available to you. It's never too early or

too late to invest. Take action in investing.

Don't just plan it and not do it. Don't put it

off any longer. Just remember that

knowledge plus wisdom equates to power;

power to attract money; power that controls

your life; power that keeps you motivated to

achieve your goals; and power that leads

you on the right path to financial freedom.

USING MONEY WISELY

Most of us spend more money when we

make more money. This is a critical

mistake. You should learn to economize

and save up your income for future use. An

effective way to start saving is to tuck

money away in retirement accounts. True,

your paycheck will be a little smaller but you won't regret it. The money will help you when you are retired and become dependent on a fixed income. You will have the money to pay your bills and other necessities. So, start investing your money as soon as possible and put money aside in retirement funds. When it comes to money growth, time plays an important role. The more time you give your investments to grow, the more money you will have in the future.

THINK POSITIVE, NOT NEGATIVE

Our minds control our behavior, actions, and generally our lives. The wisdom and knowledge we hold is all we need to think positively and not negatively. It helps us to become optimists instead of pessimists. Believing in yourself is the only way you can succeed in anything. This includes helping us spend less money. Try to put aside as much money as possible into your retirement account(s). Try to have money set aside to invest with. Check with your

financial advisor to see what type(s) of

retirement account(s) are suitable for you.

A *401k, IRA, Roth IRA, SEP, Keogh,*

and/or *SIMPLE* retirement account is

recommended.

FACING YOUR DEBT

Being in debt is something most of us

cannot avoid. We are faced with debt

problems at point or another. You might

owe credit card companies, taxes and/or loan paybacks. It is a heavy burden you have to carry knowing you owe money. The amount of money you owe seems to grow faster than you can pay them back. There are two types of debt that people can be in. One is called personal debt, which is the money you owe your loved ones, family, and/or friend. The other type of debt is called institutional debt where you owe money to credit companies, bank, *IRS*, business and so on.

Whether it is personal and/or institutional debt, you must face your debt head on. Otherwise, it will become harder and more difficult to pay back those persons and/or institutions. And remember, you must pay them back! If you don't, you will be disrespecting your money and consequently yourself making it even harder to get out of debt. It's important to acknowledge your debt and not just ignore it. There are non-profit credit counselors available who can help you if you need or want one.

Take one step at a time. Take small steps in reducing your debt. Don't overwhelm yourself. You can call the institutions and/or people you owe money to and ask them to lower your interest rates. Pay a little bit than then the minimum due each month and it will greatly reduce the total interest payments you need to pay off your debt. The more you owe, the longer it will take you to repay it. So, reduce the amount you owe by paying a bit more each month and you will be one step closer to being debt free.

TRUST AND BELIEVE IN YOURSELF

Sometime others can easily influence one's behavior and decisions. Others' advice can steer you the wrong way and make things worse for you. So one of the crucial elements you have to remember in order to be on the road to financial freedom is to learn to trust and believe in yourself. If the stock or fund you invested in goes down in price, don't panic. Don't sell that stock or fund right away for it will hurt you in the long run. Assume that the investments you made are good ones and know that the stock market fluctuates. Believe in the decision you made and trust yourself. In order to make a solid investment, you must believe solidly in your investment as well.

The mind has natural tendency to think "I can't invest any money this month; I don't have enough money to pay the bills; I can't afford to give money to charity; and there

are so many things that I need and want."

Your mind must be able to break these

thoughts of poverty. All thoughts of

poverty are the bonds of poverty. You must

believe that you can break through these

thoughts and overcome these mental

barriers with the power of your mind and

will.

It is very important for you to accept the

fact that your money does have its ups and

downs. No matter how careful you plan

and do everything financially right, money

isn't going to behave in a way you can

predict. Sometimes you'll have more than

you expect and sometimes you'll have less

than you thought. Take a long look at your

financial future and follow the steps

outlined in this book. The setbacks you

may have will not keep you from financial

freedom. Create everything that is within

your power. Believe that you can do

anything and you will. Think positive, not

negative. Knowledge, wisdom, self-discipline and self-confidence are what truly create financial freedom. Respect yourself and your money. Let time create your fortunes. If you are strong enough to face your debts and your misfortunes then take action now. This will lead you on the path to financial freedom.

ANTHONY K. MARCUS

CHAPTER FOUR

YOUR LIFE, YOUR CHOICE

OVERCOMING OBSTACLES

L ife is unpredictable and filled with uncertainty. Anything can happen while on your path to financial freedom.

Achieving you goals smoothly and successfully is one of the hardest things to do. In fact, there tends to be obstacles you have to overcome. These roadblocks can become disorienting and quite confusing. It can slow down your progress and change the way you live your life.

When unforeseen obstacles happen, don't be discouraged. Don't assume that you are not worthy of achieving your goals. Have faith in yourself. Don't undermine your own wits. You must believe that you are able to overcome any obstacles in your way. Allow yourself to be more flexible in order to consciously handle the unexpected.

While on the path to achieving your goals, you will grow in ways that you have never imagined. You will become wiser than ever before. To reach your goals, you may need to do things differently than what you have done before. You have to be optimistic and be open to various ideas and concepts. You must expect the unexpected. Take advantage of any assistance that may cross your path.

A goal is like a dream, a dream that you create and push forward. While pursuing your dream, you will change. You will see a natural exciting circle of growth. The strength to achieve your dreams comes from the will power within you. Pursue your dreams and follow your heart. Let your mind be shaped by your goals.

STRIVING TOWARDS SUCCESS

We all live in an economic-based world.

We need to take responsibility for not only

ourselves but also others in order to achieve

the level of financial freedom we want. If

we want to eliminate our exposure to

economic crisis and build a strong financial

future to our loved ones and ourselves then

we need to take charge and take

responsibility. We all need to keep in mind

that having financial freedom is not the

judge of our net worth but our self-worth.

We do not live our lives by just

accumulating wealth and spending money.

Our quality of life is defined by who we are

as an individual. We are not defined by

what we have or do not have. True

financial freedom requires having the

money to care for yourself and the people

you care for.

By reading this book, you have gained the

knowledge and self-confidence to master

your finances. By pursuing your dreams

and overcoming your fears you can do

anything you put your mind to. This

includes gaining your financial freedom. Let us walk together onto the path to financial freedom. **God bless you.**

SUMMARY

It is known that many people all around the world are in financial debt. Most of them do not know how to free themselves from such debt and many end up in financial ruin. *How to Take the Path to Financial Freedom* describes just how to overcome tremendous obstacles to get rid of financial debt. This book shows how

putting one's family and loved ones above

their financial burdens can lead a person out

of debt. It tells people how to lay out a

foundation in accumulating wealth and

leading them out of having to worry about

the future of themselves and their loved

ones. This useful and handy financial guide

approaches the subject in both practical and

spiritual ways. Being in debt now doesn't

necessarily mean that a person has to be in

debt forever. People do have the power to

climb out of debt if they truly want to.

ABOUT THE AUTHOR

Anthony K. Marcus is a freelance writer who was born in Singapore. He graduated at England's School of Business in London with a MBA degree. He migrated to the United States in 1987 and now resides in California.

Mr. Marcus has a vast experience in personal finance. All the concepts in this book was created and refined by him. He is now writing his new book *Journey To The*

Gambling World that is due to be out in the

spring or early summer of 2004.

www.ingramcontent.com/pod-product-compliance
Lightning Source LLC
Chambersburg PA
CBHW020351290526
45785CB00005B/2233